CALVIN AND HOBBES
SUNDAY PAGES 1985-1995

An Exhibition Catalogue by

BILL WATTERSON

**Andrews McMeel
Publishing**

Kansas City

In cooperation with
The Ohio State University
Cartoon Research Library

07 08 MPT 5 4

Library of Congress Cataloging-in-Publication Data
Watterson, Bill.
[Calvin and Hobbes. Selections]
Calvin and Hobbes : Sunday papers, 1985-1995 / Bill Watterson.
p. cm.
Catalog of an exhibition held Sept. 10, 2001 to Jan. 16, 2002 at the Ohio State University Cartoon Research Library.
Highlights 36 Sunday cartoons that the author has personally selected from his collection.
ISBN-13: 978-0-7407-2135-9
ISBN-10: 0-7407-2135-6
1. Watterson, Bill. Calvin and Hobbes–Exhibitions. 2. Watterson, Bill–Exhibitions. I. Title

PN6728.C34W385162001
741.5'973–dc21   2001046405

Design: Frank Pauer

This catalogue accompanies the exhibition *Calvin and Hobbes: Sunday Pages 1985-1995* at The Ohio State University Cartoon Research Library from September 10, 2001, to January 15, 2002.

The exhibition was mounted with the support of The Ohio State University Libraries. All works in the exhibition are from the personal collection of the cartoonist, and we are grateful to him for lending them for this purpose. We also appreciate the contributions of Frank Pauer, Marilyn Scott, Erin Shipley, Dennis Toth, Rick VanBrimmer, and Richard Samuel West to the exhibit and this publication. Special thanks to Andrews McMeel Publishing for producing and distributing this book.

Cover: [unpublished watercolor of Calvin and Hobbes] Private collection. Watercolor on paper. 12 x 12.4 cm.

PREFACE

Everyone misses *Calvin and Hobbes*.

It reinvented the newspaper comic strip at a time when many had all but buried the funnies as a vehicle for fresh, creative work. Then Bill Watterson came along and reminded a new generation of what older readers and comic strip afficionados knew: A well-written and beautifully drawn strip is an intricate, powerful form of communication. And with *Calvin and Hobbes*, we had fun—just like readers of *Krazy Kat* and *Pogo* did. Opening the newspaper each day was an adventure. The heights of Watterson's creative imagination took us places we had never been. We miss that.

This book is published in conjunction with the first exhibition of original *Calvin and Hobbes* Sunday pages at The Ohio State University Cartoon Research Library. Although the work was created for reproduction, not for gallery display, it is a pleasure to see the cartoonist's carefully placed lines and exquisite brush strokes. In an attempt to share this experience with those who are unable to visit the exhibition, all of the original Sunday pages displayed are reproduced in color in this book so that every detail, such as sketch lines, corrections, and registration marks, are visible. On the opposite page the same comic strip is printed in full color. Because Watterson was unusually intentional and creative in his use of color, this juxtaposition provides *Calvin and Hobbes* readers the opportunity to consider the impact of color on its narrative and content.

When I first contacted Bill Watterson about the possibility of exhibiting his original work, I used the term "retrospective." He replied that we might be able to do an exhibit, but that calling it a retrospective made him uncomfortable since it has been only a few years since he stopped drawing the comic strip. He felt that a longer time was needed to put *Calvin and Hobbes* in the historical perspective implied by that term. Nonetheless, this show is a "look back" at the comic strip as we revisit favorites that we remember. *Calvin and Hobbes: Sunday Pages 1985-1995* is particularly interesting because each work that is included was selected by Bill Watterson. His comments about the thirty-six Sunday pages he chose are part of this volume. In addition, he reflects on *Calvin and Hobbes* from the perspective of six years, and his essay provides insights into his life as a syndicated cartoonist.

Reprint books of *Calvin and Hobbes* are nice to have, but the opportunity to see the original work and read Bill Watterson's thoughts about it is a privilege. He generously shared not only the art, but also his time and his thoughts. When I first reviewed the works included in the exhibit, I knew that everyone who visited it would begin with laughter and end with tears.

On behalf of all who enjoyed *Calvin and Hobbes*, thank you, Bill Watterson.

Lucy Shelton Caswell
Professor and Curator
The Ohio State University Cartoon Research Library
June 2001

21

More Facts

- Sphynx cats were originally called Canadian Hairless Cats. **Breeders** agreed on the new name after comparing the cat to a **mythological** creature called a Sphinx.

- Hairlessness is a **recessive gene**. So Sphynx cats came into this world by accident. The first Canadian Hairless Cat was born in Toronto. Its name was Prune.

- Sphynx cats get cold easily. They don't have hair to keep them warm. Sweaters or cuddling can help!

Glossary

breeder – a person who raises animals primarily for breeding purposes.

fine – very thin.

mythological – imaginary.

pattern – a repeated marking.

recessive gene – a gene that causes a characteristic in offspring only if both parents have it.

wrinkles – small lines or folds that appear on the skin.

Index

abdokids.com

Use this code to log on to abdokids.com and access crafts, games, videos and more!

Abdo Kids Code:
CSK9237

3 1333 04633 8230